FREIGHTLINER LOCOMOTIVES

Dave Smith

AMBERLEY

Front Cover: No. 47270 *Cory Brothers* heads north at Kangaroo Spinney, Wellingborough, with 6M26 – the 14.05 Dagenham to Crewe Gresty Lane Ford cars/vans, on 9 April 2003.

Rear Cover: No. 66553 waits to depart Croft Sidings in Leicestershire with 6M17 – the 1017 Croft to Neasden loaded aggregates, on 9 March 2007.

First published 2020

Amberley Publishing
The Hill, Stroud
Gloucestershire, GL5 4EP

www.amberley-books.com

Copyright © Dave Smith, 2020

The right of Dave Smith to be identified as the Author of this work has been asserted in accordance with the Copyright, Designs and Patents Act 1988.

ISBN 978 1 4456 7370 7 (print)
ISBN 978 1 4456 7371 4 (ebook)

British Library Cataloguing in Publication Data.
A catalogue record for this book is available from the British Library.

Origination by Amberley Publishing.
Printed in the UK.

Introduction

When Freightliner was privatised back in 1996, it then only operated intermodal container services. These ran from ports including Felixstowe, Southampton and Tilbury, to terminals in Birmingham (Lawley Street), Manchester (Trafford Park), Bristol (Ashton Gate), and Wentloge–Newport, South Wales. Today, Coatbridge in Scotland, Daventry (DIRFT), and Garston are all major terminals, and service an extensive road distribution network with over 300 road vehicles. The company's traction fleet upon privatisation consisted of ten Class 08 shunting locomotives, thirty Class 47s, twenty Class 86 electric locomotives, and ten relatively new Class 90s. In 1997 the company commissioned a rebuild of six of its Class 47s to create the Class 57s, with reconditioned General Motors 645 power units, with only the body shells and bogies from the Class 47s. This work took place by Brush at Loughborough, with the first loco entering service in the summer of 1998. With the first batch of Class 57s performing well, six more were ordered in 1999 bring the total to twelve. In the same year Freightliner set up Heavy Haul, which started by operating railway infrastructure trains for Network Rail moving ballast and rails, before moving into the bulk loads market. By the spring of 1999, Freightliner ordered the first five Class 66s off the General Motors production line at London Ontario for shipping to Newport docks.

It wasn't long before Freightliner ordered more, mainly for additional work with the Railtrack business, and new commercial freight flows being cement from Hope, and as a replacement for the ageing Class 47s on intermodal traffic. By the end of 2000, Nos 66506 to 66525 were all in service. By 2007 the Class 66 deliveries reached a point where the Class 57 locomotives were no longer required, and Freightliner handed all twelve back to the leasing company, Porterbrook. Also in 2007, the company commissioned General Electric to produce thirty diesel locomotives on a new design. They were built in Erie, Pennsylvania, with the first two completed examples, Nos 70001 and 70002, tested in the USA in July 2009, before shipping to the UK in November 2009. With more to follow in 2012, the fleet size would have been twenty, but unfortunately No. 70012 was dropped during unloading and had to be returned to the USA.

The introduction of the Class 70s released a number of Class 66s for use in Poland, for its fast-growing operations, while nine Class 66s, Nos 66573 to 66581, were returned to the leasing company. Then, in late 2011, Freightliner took on the lease of ten former Direct Rail Services locomotives, Nos 66411 to 66420, some of which now work in Poland. With Freightliner renewing its mainline diesel fleet, there was no change to its electric locomotives classes 86s and 90s that the company inherited for use on the West Coast Mainline and in East Anglia. Moving forward to February 2015, Freightliner was sold to Genesee & Wyoming, a short line railroad holding company that owns or maintains an interest in over 120 railroads in no fewer than seven countries: the USA, Canada, Austria, Belgium, The Netherlands, Poland and the United Kingdom.

Class 47s

Back in May 1997 Freightliner named Class 47 No. 47114 *Freightlinerbulk* to mark the opening of the new Thames Freightliner terminal, at the same time promoting the company credentials for moving bulk commodities by ISO tank containers. The loco received its new two-tone green livery incorporating the italicised freightliner name and red triangle. On 23 March 2001, No. 47114 heads north at Helpston with a very short 4E62 – the 04.41 Felixstowe–Leeds service.

The freightliner-liveried Class 47s were a rare sight on the Midland main line. Here we see No. 47150 passing Irchester on the Up/Down slow line, working 4M26 – the 14.26 Dagenham–Crewe Gresty lane – on 6 May 2003. The load consists of Ford Transit and Fiesta models eventually bound for Garston distribution terminal.

With the oilseed rape in full flower, No. 47150 heads north at Easenhall on the west coast main line dragging Pendolino No. 390001 as 4X70 Wembley–Old Dalby for testing on 23 April 2003.

Courteenhall on the Northampton loop is the location, as No. 47197 continues its climb up from the county town with a well-loaded 4L67 – the 16.45 Lawley St–Ipswich yard service – on 4 April 2001.

Sporting Freightliner's early grey livery No. 47197 passes Ashton in Northamptonshire working 4X71 – the 07.32 Old Dalby–Wembley, dragging Pendolino No. 390011 – on 13 April 2001.

The single line on the Hoo Junction–Isle of Grain branch passes through the village of Cliffe. Here we see No. 47212 pass with 4088 – the 05.32 Crewe Basford Hall–Thamesport service – on 7 April 2001.

Catching the early morning sun on 6 January 2001, a tatty-looking No. 47224 heads south, at Claydon, to the north of Banbury, working 4014 – the 06.52 Crewe Basford Hall–Southampton service.

With the first General Motors Class 66s being delivered for Freightliner in July 1999, the ageing Class 47s were becoming surplus to requirements. Here we see, in Basford Hall yard at Crewe, on 17 April 2003, no fewer than seven, Nos 47258/114/234/353/308/290 and 193, awaiting their fate.

Being named *Cory Brothers 1842–1992* at Tinsley Traction & Maintenance depot, in September 1996, No. 47270 passes Wellingborough working 6M26 – the 14.05 Dagenham–Crewe Gresty lane Ford cars – on 9 April 2003. The loco was stored in January 2005 at Crewe Basford Hall, then purchased by T. J. Thompson & Sons for scrapping in early March 2007. By the end of March of the same year, the locomotive had been secured for preservation moving to the Nene Valley Railway. Today the loco still survives and is owned and operated by West Coast Railways ltd.

Captured two months into its preservation, No. 47270 *Cory Brothers 1842–1992* is seen at Wansford station during the Nene Valley Railways Royal Mail weekend on 24 June 2007.

Now preserved at the Great Central Railway north, No. 47292 heads up through Moorgates on the North Yorkshire Moors Railway top-and-tailed with No. 57304 working the 14.50 service from Grosmont–Pickering, on 12 April 2003, during the line's diesel gala. At the time the loco was still in service with Freightliner and was a guest visitor for the weekend.

Two different liveries are contrasted as Nos 47289, in grey, with 47150, in green, pass Elford, to the north of Tamworth, working 4031 – the 14.33 Leeds–Southampton service – on 31 January 2001.

Six years on from the previous picture, No. 47289 heads a line-up of stored locomotives at Crewe Basford Hall yard awaiting their fate with Nos 86623/47302/86635/633 and 86602 on 9 February 2006.

Grimsbury, to the north of Banbury, is the setting as No. 47334 *P&O Nedlloyd* heads south working 4014 – the 06.52 Crewe Basford Hall–Southampton service – on 26 January 2001.

On a cold, crisp snow-covered 30 December 2000, No. 47358 passes South Moreton on the Great Western main line working No. 4024 – the 09.36 Crewe Basford Hall–Southampton Freightliner service.

Playing host to a Freightliner double, Newport station in south Wales sees Nos 47367 and 47290 passing through the middle road working 4V16 – the 09.46 Millbrook–Cardiff Pengam service – on 6 November 1999.

No. 47376, in original freightliner livery, was used to launch the company in 1995, being named *Freightliner 1995*. Now preserved on the Gloucestershire & Warwickshire Railway, it's seen on 29 December 2013 as it passes Hailes Abbey with 2C22 – the 12.00 Laverton–Cheltenham service.

Still sporting its old Virgin Trains colours, No. 47812, with Freightliner branding, departs Hornsey depot dragging 317315 as 5Z12 – the 14.19 to Bedford Cauldwell walk depot – on 19 November 2004.

Lidlington on the Bedford–Bletchley branch is the location as Nos 47816 and 47811, both in their First Great Western green, head 5Z10 – the Rugby–Bedford Cauldwell walk depot barrier move – on 11 April 2005.

No. 47829 was painted into Police livery in 2002 as part of a rail safety campaign launched by the British Transport Police. It was named at Birmingham International on 25 March of that year. In the hands of Freightliner, here we see the loco heading north at Ashton, working 4M26 – the 14.05 Dagenham–Crewe Basford Hall Ford cars – on 19 June 2003.

In 2006, Freightliner were contracted by Southern Railways to move its Class 456 electric units to Wolverton works for overhaul/rebranding from NSE to the Southern green livery. On 30 April 2007, No. 47830 heads through Willesden Brent dragging 456007 as 5Z19 from Selhurst depot–Wolverton works.

After being named in 1965, No. D1679, now 47843 *Vulcan*, passes Harrowden Junction, still with the same name, with 6Z78 – the 13.05 Toton TMD–Bedford yard translator move on 2 September 2004. This was in readiness for the then unit moves for Thameslink to and from Selhurst and Hornsey depots during their London blockade.

With some of Thameslink's Class 319s running under their own power from Selhurst to Bletchley, here we see, on 29 November 2004, No. 319374 after arriving before No. 47843, which was attached to form 5X54 to Bedford.

Corby Euro Terminal is the setting as No. 47848, named *Newton Abbot Festival of Transport*, helps failed Class 66 No. 66603 with coolant problems, as they wait to depart with 4X43 – the 18.00 Ford cars to Crewe Basford Hall – on 31 July 2003.

Class 57s

On 2 March 2002, Pathfinder Tours ran a Railtour in memory of Freightliner driver Steve Dunn, who sadly lost his life in the railway accident at Great Heck, near Selby, on 28 February 2001. Here we see No. 57005 *Freightliner Excellence* with 1Z57 on the Crewe to Sheffield leg, where it was replaced by No. 66601 at York.

Looked on by the then fully operational Didcot power station, No. 57006 *Freightliner Reliance* heads a well-loaded 4002 – the 09.47 Lawley St–Southampton service through Moreton cutting – on 13 July 2001.

No. 57008 *Freightliner Explorer* heads south at Grimsbury to the north of Banbury with 4017 – the 15.52 Lawley St–Southampton Freightliner – on 7 June 2004.

Kennet in East Anglia is the setting as No. 57010 *Freightliner Crusader* heads east with a short/lightly loaded 4L89 – the 22.00 Coatbridge–Ipswich yard service – on 31 July 2004.

Powering away from a signal check at Rugby station, on a cold 6 February 2007, is No. 57010 *Freightliner Crusader* working 4L93 – the 10.08 Lawley St–Felixstowe Freightliner.

No. 57011 *Freightliner Challenger* climbs up from Northampton at Wilsons crossing in Kingsthorpe working 4M81 – the 10.44 Ipswich yard–Trafford Park service – on 16 October 2003.

With the May trees in full blossom, one of freightliner's ex-DRS Class 66s, still in its old colours, No. 66413, heads east at Kirby Bellars on the Leicester–Peterborough line on 21 May 2018. It is working 4L93 – the 10.30 Lawley St–Felixstowe North service.

Looking a lot smarter in its new Genesee & Wyoming company colours, No. 66413 passes the western Northamptonshire village of King's Sutton on 2 August 2018. It is working a lightly loaded 4M67 – the 14.17 Southampton–Hams Hall service.

Still sporting its blue colours when in Stobart livery for DRS, No. 66414 passes Copleys Brook, Melton Mowbray, with a well-loaded 4M20 – the 10.14 Felixstowe–Lawley St diverted Freightliner service – on 17 May 2014.

In the early hours of 24 March 2019, No. 66414, now in its new Powerhaul livery, is seen in an engineering possession at Hayes & Harlington with 6Y40 – the 21.33 from Hinksey yard.

A tatty-looking No. 66418, still in blue, passes Didcot East Junction on 13 December 2014 working a shorter than usual 4O14 – the 07.37 Hams Hall–Southampton Freightliner.

Now looking a lot smarter in its Powerhaul livery, No. 66418 heads south at Soulbury on the WCML, working a well-loaded 4O13 – the 12.06 Daventry (DIRFT) reception–Southampton service – on 26 February 2016.

Captured while in an engineering possession at Roade, No. 66419, still in its blue livery, is seen with 6Y16 loaded ballast from Crewe Basford Hall on 21 September 2014.

Catching the early evening sun as it passes Quadring, on 15 May 2019, No. 66419, in its new Genesee & Wyoming livery, heads 4E56 – the 15.46 Felixstowe North FLT–Doncaster Railport service.

Class 66/5s

Heading east on the Great Western main line at Compton Beauchamp, No. 66501 *Japan 2001* passes, working a short 4L31 – the 09.03 Bristol Freight terminal–Felixstowe service – on 16 April 2014.

Passing through the centre roads at Leamington Spa station, No. 66502 *Basford Hall Centenary 2001* heads 4M28 – the 09.32 Southampton–Ditton service – on 20 January 2016.

A work-stained Powerhaul-liveried No. 66504 heads along the Gospel Oak–Barking line at Leyton Midland road, in East London, working 4L52 – the 03.25 Garston–London Gateway service – on 14 February 2019.

Heading south on the joint line at Donington in Lincolnshire, No. 66515 heads 4L87 – the 08.51 Leeds–Felixstowe North service – on 13 September 2018.

Normally working during the hours of darkness, the Sussex draintrain, seen in daylight hours at Northampton station with Nos 66519 and 66511, is ready to depart back to Bletchley yard as 6Y70 – the 10.30 departure – on 2 August 2004.

Manea located in East Anglia, still with its semaphore signals, is the setting as No. 66520 passes through at speed with 4L93 – the 10.08 Lawley St–Felixstowe service – on 25 September 2018.

Easing out of Eggborough power station, at Whitley bridge junction, on 3 March 2015, No. 66526 *Driver Steve Dunn (George)* departs with 4R37 – the 15.18 empty coal working to Immingham.

Since taking this picture back on 2 February 2013, much has changed with loco No. 66527 *Don Raider*, now working for Freightliner in Poland and the Euro Terminal at Willesden (closed for the HS2 project). Here we see the loco between shunt moves with the HOBC train.

The freight-only line from Sheet Stores Junction–Stenson Junction is the setting as No. 66533 *Hanjin Express* passes under the M1 motorway at Lockington working 6G65 – the 09.19 Hope Earles Sidings–Walsall Freight Terminal loaded cement-conveying thirty-six PCA tanks on 15 February 2019.

The cross-country route via Ely is an obvious choice for trains between Yorkshire and the east coast port of Felixstowe, with its great backdrop of its cathedral. No. 66540 *Ruby* takes the line to Chippenham Junction at Ely, working 4L87 – the 08.51 service from Leeds – on 5 April 2019.

Catching the early morning sun, No. 66545 passes Wetmore farm, Burton Upon Trent, working 6M66 – the 03.49 Immingham–Rugeley power station loaded coal on 25 November 2008.

Looked on by both Ferrybridge power station and Kellingley colliery, No. 66547 heads east at Whitley bridge on 3 March 2015 working 6R08 – the 10.10 Sudforth lane–Eggborough power station loaded coal.

Under threatening skies, No. 66553 heads north at Cathiron on the WCML, working 6Z36 – the 14.05 Dagenham–Crewe Gresty lane Ford cars/vans – on 23 June 2003.

Heading along the then single Up/Down slow line at Irchester, No. 66554 passes the old station and goods shed with 6L45 – the 07.35 Hope Earles Sidings–West Thurrock loaded cement – on 6 March 2009. Since taking this shot, an extra line has been added along with overhead electrification masts, which will extend the electrification from Bedford to Corby.

Being over seven hours late made this shot possible at this location. No. 66555 passes the North Bedfordshire village of Souldrop with 6C51 – the 10.25 Forders Sidings–Cricklewood loaded binliner – on 14 June 2004.

The busy fuel depot at Freightliner's Ipswich stabling point is supplied from Lindsey Oil refinery once a week by rail. Here we see No. 66556 passing Pochins crossing at Rearsby with 6E50 – the 10.27 Ipswich S.S.– Lindsey – on 20 December 2016.

No. 66558 is seen arriving at Stud Farm Quarry, in Leicestershire, on the branch from Bagworth Junction, on 24 January 2007, with 6F12 empty ballast wagons from Forders Sidings.

Kangaroo Spinney, at Wellingborough, on the MML is the setting as No. 66560 heads north on 29 September 2014 with 6D45 – the 15.39 Luton Crescent Road–Mountsorrel, conveying JNA wagons.

Captured inside Bletchley TMD, No. 66562 is seen running around its barrier wagons after arriving with 7X33 from Derby Litchurch Lane. It is with new electric unit No. 387205, for the Gatwick Express, on 20 November 2015.

Passing Croxton Limeworks in North Lincolnshire on 2 November 2018, No. 66563 heads 6C75 – the 10.55 loaded coal working from Immingham–Scunthorpe, where it is used in the TATA steelworks.

Catching the early evening sun at King's Sutton to the south of Banbury, No. 66564 heads north with 6M28 – the 18.16 Hinksey Yard–Bescot engineers working on 22 July 2014.

Heading east at Syston, in Leicestershire, No. 66566 is seen working a well-loaded diverted 4L97 – the 04.57 Trafford Park–Felixstowe freightliner service – on 17 May 2014.

Taking a break from its usual intermodal duties, No. 66572 is seen in Camden carriage sidings, on 6 January 2019, with an engineers train – 6Y58 – of loaded ballast working from Crewe Basford Hall.

Now with GBRF and renumbered 66739 with the name *Bluebell Railway*, No. 66579 passes through Northampton station with 4O86 – the 07.25 Crewe Basford Hall–Grain service – on 1 May 2007.

After negotiating the steep climb up from Market Harborough, No. 66581 *Sophie* passes Desborough working 6M17 – the 10.17 Croft Sidings–Neasden aggregates – on 18 October 2007. This loco is also in the hands of GBRF and renumbered 66741 being named *Swanage Railway*.

Wolverton centre sidings is the setting as No. 66585 *The Drax Flyer* is captured after arriving with 5Z80 from Eastleigh, conveying unit Nos 442421 and 442424 for refurb, on 17 April 2008.

To celebrate a new contract with container shipping firm Ocean Network Express (One), Freightliner has repainted No. 66587 into One's magenta colours with the name *As One, We Can*. Here we see the loco passing Werrington on 14 June 2019 working 4L53 – the 16.30 Doncaster Europort–Felixstowe Freightliner service.

Now fully electrified, the well-photographed location of Sonning cutting is the setting as No. 66588 heads an eastbound 4L31 – the 09.03 Bristol–Felixstowe FLT service – on 22 April 2015.

Mechanical signalling has survived into the twenty-first century at the fenland town of Whittlesea. Here we see No. 66589 working a diverted 4L90 – the 08.57 Lawley St–Felixstowe FLT – on 15 September 2012.

Captured at Crewe Basford Hall on 29 April 2007, only eight days after arriving into the UK from the General Motors/EMD plant at London, Ontario, in Canada, Nos 66592 and 66587 wait to enter service for Freightliner.

Heading a colourful/well-loaded 4O95 – the 12.12 Leeds–Southampton service – on 17 January 2019, No. 66593 *3MG Mersey Multimodal Gateway* is seen heading south through Trowell Junction.

On a cold, crisp 4 February 2009, No. 66595 passes Souldrop working 6L45 – the 07.35 Hope Earles Sidings–West Thurrock loaded cement. Since taking this picture the slow lines are now doubled and electrified.

Class 66/6s

With the Rosebay Willowherb in full bloom, No. 66601 *The Hope Valley* passes through Wymington in north Bedfordshire with 6D45 – the 15.52 Luton Crescent Road–Mountsorrel self-discharge empties – on 17 July 2015.

Catching some early spring sunshine, No. 66602 heads south at Rushton working 6Y77 – the 08.41 Toton North Yard–Hendon engineers – on 24 March 2019.

Brinklow on the WCML sees No. 66603 heading north with 6M51 – the 14.15 Stewarts Lane Tarmac–
Tunstead Sidings empties – on 31 July 2018.

After passing the site of the disused station at Great Oakley on the Manton–Kettering line, No. 66604 heads
a new set of VTG 100-tonne JPA wagons, built in Germany by Feldbinder, on 6V94 – the 07.35 Hope Earles
Sidings–Theale loaded cement – on 4 December 2015.

Crossing the river Great Ouse, No. 66605 is seen on Sharnbrook viaduct heading south with 6V94 – the 07.35 Hope Earles Sidings–Theale cement – conveying thirty-six PCAs on 25 July 2014.

With Ratcliffe power station clear in the distance No. 66606 heads through Castle Donnington with 6M49 – the 07.45 Immingham–Rugeley 'B' power station loaded coal – on 30 September 2015. Just under nine months later, Rugeley 'B' closed on 8 June 2016 due to a fall in market prices and increasing carbon costs, with demolition due for completion by spring 2019.

No. 66607 departs Bedford after a crew change heading north with 6M91 – the 14.08 Theale–Hope Earles Sidings – on 10 May 2017.

With No. 66608 now working for Freightliner in Poland (FPL) and renumbered 66603, we see it in the company of CTL's M62Y-375 and Kolprems EU07-158, all stabled up at Dabrowa Gornicza Zabkowice on 9 June 2017.

Winwick Junction is the setting as No. 66610 passes with 6E40 – the 15.20 MWF only Stanlow–Humber bogie pressure tanks – on 18 July 2003.

Without its Freightliner bodyside brandings, No. 66612 *Forth Raider* heads north at Wellingborough with 6Z54 – the 12.30 Thorney Mill–Bardon Hill empties – on 17 May 2005. In July 2011, this loco was exported to Poland via Immingham docks and now carries the number 66606.

A new flow for Freightliner in 2018 was the transporting of aviation fuel to serve Heathrow Airport in London. Under threatening skies, on 16 October 2018, No. 66613 passes through Kensington Olympia with 6O08 – the 12.55 Colnbrook Baa Logistics–Grain Oil Terminal empties.

Seen sporting Freightliner's new branding with Genesee & Wyoming is No. 66614 *Poppy 1916–2016* named in memory of fifteen brave lads from Buxton Lime firms, who gave their lives at the Batttle of the Somme. It is seen climbing away from Wellingborough with 6L44 – the 05.21 Tunstead–West Thurrock loaded cement on – 30 November 2018.

No. 66615 rolls into Mantle Lane, Coalville, for a crew change working 6Z44 – the 03.48 York South Yard–Bardon Hill, where the train was loaded with aggregates for Chesterton Junction – on 26 March 2018.

The north Bedfordshire village of Souldrop is the setting on 16 August 2017 as No. 66616 heads north with 6M84 – the 14.08 Dagenham Down Yard–Hope Earles Sidings empties.

A rare visitor to the Colas Depot at Rugby sees No. 66617, inside the service/maintenance shed, collecting part of the HOBC as the 6Z25 to Crewe Basford Hall on 3 February 2010.

No. 66618 *Railways Illustrated Annual Photographic Awards* heads north at Souldrop on the MML working 6M91 – the 11.13 Theale–Hope Earles Sidings – on 8 June 2016.

Irchester plays host to a work-stained No. 66619 *Derek W. Johnson MBE* as it passes with 6M84 – the 12.40 Marks Tey Tarmac–Barrow Hill Up sidings – on 22 September 2016.

Passing its fine array of semaphores signals at Langham Junction, on the Leicester–Peterborough line, No. 66620 heads 6L89 – the 11.49 Tunstead–West Thurrock – on 24 March 2014.

Crossing the river Nene at Irchester, No. 66621 climbs up from Wellingborough working 6L88 – the 07.10 Bardon Hill–Bow aggregates – on 29 October 2008. The wagons are KEAs which started life as Channel Tunnel segment wagons operated by TML (Transmarche-Link).

In a lucky patch of winter sun on 7 February 2017, No. 66622 heads along the C2C mainline through Rainham working 6L44 – the 05.22 Tunstead Sidings–West Thurrock loaded cement.

Back in 2006 Freightliner Heavyhaul gained a five-year contract with Aggregate Industries taking over all regular flows from Bardon Hill. In 2007 the company painted loco No. 66623 in Bardon Aggregate blue livery and named it *Bill Bolsover*. Here we see the loco passing Wellingborough on 24 September 2014 working 6M79 – the 11.56 Angerstein Wharf–Bardon Hill using Freightliner's own HIA wagons.

Still retaining its *Bill Bolsover* name but losing its Aggregates branding for the newer Freightliner logo, No. 66623 passes Irchester working 6D45 – the 15.52 Luton Crescent Road–Mountsorrel self-discharge empties – on 15 May 2015.

Looking smart in its new colours, No. 66623, the second loco to carry the livery of Freightliner's parent company, Genesee & Wyoming, passes Cooks Lane, Kilby Bridge, working 6M91 – the 11.13 Theale–Hope Earles Sidings – on 1 April 2019.

Seen only two weeks after being delivered, No. 66624 waits to depart Croft Sidings, in Leicestershire, on 5 March 2007, with its new rake of HIA hoppers as 6M17 – the 10.17 to Neasden, in London.

No. 66624 is seen in Luton Crescent road yard with the self-discharge train after arriving from Mountsorrel as 6C79 on 20 May 2009. This loco was new to Freightliner in 2007 and in June 2010 moved to Freightliner PL, in Poland, from Immingham Docks and now has the new number of 66602.

No. 66625 unloads its train over the BDU at London concretes plant, at Neasden, after arriving with 6M25 from Croft Quarry, in Leicestershire, on 19 June 2008. This locomotive was exported to Poland during October 2009 and works for Freightliner PL and was renumbered 66601.

Elstow's Tarmac terminal to the south of Bedford is the location as No. 66951 heads round from the BDU unloading aggregates after arriving with 6Z16 – the 05.45 working from Crewe Basford Hall – on 2 February 2012.

Now working in Poland for Freightliner, No. 66954 heads south at Gordons Lodge, Ashton, with 4L41 – the 06.04 Crewe Basford Hall–Felixstowe FLT service – on 26 August 2016.

Under threatening skies, No. 66955 top-and-tailed with No. 66526 *Driver Steve Dunn (George)* as they wait in the middle road at Rhyl station to enter an engineering possession on 5 November 2017. This was 6Y55 – the 20.32 loaded ballast from Crewe Basford Hall.

No. 66957 *Stephenson's Locomotive Society 1909–2009* catches the early morning sun as it passes Old Lindslade with a very short/diverted 6Z26 – the 05.09 Bescot Up Engineers yard–Eastleigh East yard engineers – on 12 August 2016.

Looked on by the now closed and recently demolished Didcot power station, No. 70001 *Powerhaul* heads a colourful 4O27 – the 05.26 Garston–Southampton service through Moreton Cutting – on 29 March 2014.

Cathiron in Warwickshire is the location as No. 70002 heads for Daventry International Railfreight Terminal (DIRFT) with 4Z27 – the 05.25 intermodal service from Coatbridge F.L.T. – on 12 May 2016.

Heading along the Stenson Junction–Sheetstores Junction line at Chellaston on 26 April 2013, No. 70003 passes with 6M36 – the 03.21 Liverpool Bulk Terminal–Ratcliffe power station loaded coal.

Barrow-Upon-Soar on the MML is the location for No. 70004 *The Coal Industry Society* as it passes with 6L89 – the 12.35 Tunstead–West Thurrock loaded cement – on 5 July 2013.

With its well-loaded and colourful train, No. 70005 heads through Barrow-Upon-Trent with 4O95 – the 12.13 Leeds–Southampton service – on 9 September 2017.

Passing the site of Finedon Sidings on the Midland main line, No. 70006 heads 6V94 – the 07.35 Hope Earles Sidings–Theale cement-conveying thirty-six loaded PCA wagons on 24 October 2013.

With the electrification mast bases evident, No. 70007 passes Denchworth on the GW main line with a well-loaded 4090 – the 09.58 Wentlog–Southampton Freightliner service – on 1 October 2015. Since taking this picture the electrification is complete and fully operational.

Looked on by the now demolished Didcot power station, No. 70008 heads 4027 – the 05.26 Garston–Southampton service – as it passes South Moreton on 22 February 2014.

With Didcot power station in the distance, No. 70009 heads a very short and lightly loaded 4027 – the 05.21 Garston–Southampton service – through Didcot East junction on 26 September 2015.

No. 70010 heads through the village of Rearsby, in rural Leicestershire, as it passes with 4M81 – the 08.01 Felixstowe North FLT–Crewe Basford Hall service – on 15 May 2019.

Heading south on the MML at Cossington, No. 70011 passes with a well-loaded 6U77 – the 14.48 Mountsorrel–Crewe Basford Hall ballast – on 4 June 2011. This working is now in the hands of DRS.

No. 70013 arrives at Kettering station for a crew change on 5 April 2013, while working 6L87 – the 12.08 Tunstead–West Thurrock loaded cement. At the time this was a new flow for Freightliner Heavyhaul and continues to date.

Ratcliffe power station in Nottinghamshire, in the East Midlands, is the setting for No. 70014 as it's seen unloading 6D80 – the 05.01 loaded train of lime from Tunstead Sidings – on 17 July 2012.

No. 70015 working 6L87 – the 12.37 Hope Earles Sidings–West Thurrock loaded cement – passes the site of the former Glendon East Exchange Sidings, on 3 August 2012, where there was an Ironstone Quarry – previously Stewart & Lloyds Ltd. Since this photo was taken the single line is now doubled from Corby–Glendon and electrified.

Heading up into Colchester station on 2 February 2016, No. 70016 catches some winter sunshine as it passes through working 4M93 – the 13.34 Felixstowe North FLT–Lawley St service.

Still looking quaint with its old-style platform lamps, No. 70017 heads south through Leamington Spa station with 4O90 – the 06.12 Leeds–Southampton service – on 18 February 2016.

Climbing up from Ipswich on 28 January 2016, No. 70019 passes Belstead Bank with a well-loaded 4M93 – the 13.34 Felixstowe North FLT–Lawley St service.

Copley's Brook, to the west of Melton Mowbray, is the location as No. 70020 heads 4M81 – the 08.01 Felixstowe North FLT–Crewe Basford Hall service – on 19 October 2018.

Class 86s

Due to locomotive shortages, in 2002 Freightliner hired in Nos 86426 and 86430 from EWS after they had withdrawn their last examples of this class. With the contract long-term, both locos were painted in Freightliner colours. By 2004 both locos were returned to EWS and subsequently withdrawn. Here we see No. 86426 with No. 86637 as they pass Brockall on the WCML working 4L75 – the 10.14 Trafford Park–Ipswich Yard service.

Heading south at Great Brington, No. 86501 passes with a well-loaded and colourful 4L75 – the 09.58 Crewe Basford Hall–Felixstowe FLT service – on 4 June 2010.

Catching the early morning sun at Old Lindslade on the WCML, No. 86605 leads No. 86639 heading a southbound 6L89 – the 22.01 Coatbridge FLT–Felixstowe North FLT service – on 12 August 2016.

Both in Freightliner's early grey liveries Nos 86606 and 86628 head north through Tamworth station on 21 March 2003 working 4M81 – the 10.44 Ipswich Yard–Trafford Park service.

Ashton in Northamptonshire is the setting as a Freightliner treble with Nos 86609 and 86632 lead D. I. T. No. 57007 *Freightliner Bond* on 4L75 – the 10.04 Trafford Park–Ipswich Yard service – on 7 June 2005.

With its consist mainly MAERSK containers destined for the east coast port of Felixstowe, Nos 86610 and 86638 pass Chelmscote on 28 October 2011 with 4L75 – the 09.58 from Crewe Basford Hall.

With the autumn colours evident, two Freightliner grey 86s, No. 86612 *Elizabeth Garett Anderson* and No. 86606, pass Easenhall to the north of Rugby working 4L67 – the 03.30 Garston–Tilbury service – on 17 October 2003.

A colourful well-loaded 4L89 – the 22.01 Coatbridge FLT–Felixstowe North FLT – passes Gordons Lodge, Ashton, headed by Nos 86612 and 86632, on 24 May 2016.

Heading north through Castlethorpe, in Buckinghamshire, on the WCML sees Nos 86613 and 86604 working 4M87 – the 11.13 Felixstowe North–Trafford Park service – on 15 August 2019.

Pictured slightly north of the previous picture at Castlethorpe on 1 June 2003, a Freightliner triple sees Nos 86620 *Philip G. Walton* and 86610 with 66542 D. I. T. (as far as Crewe Basford Hall) heading 4M81 – the 10.44 Ipswich Yard–Trafford Park service.

Both in Freightliner's early grey livery No. 86622 leads classmate No. 86605 north past Rugby station on 30 July 2003 with a well-loaded 4M87 – the 12.49 Ipswich Yard–Trafford Park service.

Now in Powerhaul livery, No. 86622 and, in Freightliner green, No. 86613 head up into Colchester station with 4M87 – the 11.13 Felixstowe North–Trafford Park – on 2 February 2016.

A mixed treble sees Freightliner grey No. 86623 with No. 86613 and No. 57003 *Freightliner Evolution* heading south at Courtenhall, on 26 July 2002, working 4L75 – the 10.14 Trafford Park–Ipswich Yard service.

Heading a lightly loaded 4L89 – the 04.10 Crewe Basford Hall–Felixstowe North service – on 28 April 2015, Nos 86627 and 86605 pass Old Lindslade, to the north of Leighton Buzzard, in some early spring sunshine.

Fresh from the paint shops at Crewe, No. 86628 leads No. 86613 along the Oxford canal at Ansty in Warwickshire working 4M87 – the 12.49 Ipswich Yard–Trafford Park service – on 19 March 2003.

Inside the new vehicle maintenance facility (VMF) at Crewe, No. 86628 is seen during an exam with Class 90 No. 90045 receiving new brake blocks on 31 July 2018.

Waiting to enter the VMF at Crewe for component recovery, ex-Virgin trains No. 86229, then named *Lions Club International*, is seen with No. 86632, which at the time was awaiting a new transformer on 24 July 2018.

Old and new liveries are contrasted as No. 86633 *Wulfruna* and No. 86632 head south at Easenhall, on 5 November 2003, working 4L67 – the 03.30 Garston–Tilbury service – with two of Freightliner's covered car carrier wagons on the front of train.

With a very short and lightly loaded 4L75 – the 10.14 Trafford Park–Ipswich Yard service – Nos 86637 and 86627 are seen heading south at Easenhall to the north of Rugby on 24 April 2003.

Now in its new Powerhaul livery, No. 86637 leads classmate No. 86638 north at Great Brington, on 8 April 2011, working a lightly loaded 4M54 – the 10.09 Tilbury–Crewe Basford Hall service.

Class 90s

No. 90016 passes Courteenhall on the Northampton loop, working a well-loaded 4L41 – the 04.10 Crewe Basford Hall–Felixstowe North service – on 7 July 2014.

On a cold and crisp 11 January 2012, No. 90016 makes easy work of a completely empty 4L75 – the 10.14 Trafford Park–Ipswich Yard service – as it passes Church Brampton.

Heading north alongside the Oxford canal at Ansty, in Warwickshire, No. 90041 is seen working 4M88 – the 09.32 Felixstowe–Trafford Park service – on 10 October 2009.

Hired out by Freightliner to help cover the Caledonian sleeper service, No. 90041 passes Castlethorpe with 1M16 – the 20.44 Inverness–London Euston service – on 30 April 2016.

Rare visitors on the Midland main line; Nos 90041 and 90050 are pictured at West Hampstead Thameslink, on 15 August 2004, while being used to test the overheads into the then remodelled St Pancras International station.

Looked on by St Botolph's Church, dating back to the thirteenth century, in Church Brampton, No. 90042, in Powerhaul livery, heads north on 24 February with 4M88 – the 09.32 Felixstowe–Crewe Basford Hall service.

Passing through Rugby, No. 90042, in the company's early grey livery, heads north with 4M81 – the 10.44 Ipswich Yard–Trafford Park service – on 23 October 2003.

Not long after its repaint into Powerhaul livery, No. 90042 heads a colourful/well-loaded 4L41 – the 04.10 Crewe Basford Hall–Felixstowe North service at Gordons Lodge, Ashton, on 7 May 2015.

No. 90043, named *Freightliner Coatbridge*, passes Great Brington on 8 April 2011 working 4M88 – the 09.20 Ipswich Yard–Crewe Basford Hall service.

Northampton station is the setting as No. 90044 heads south on 1 May 2013 with 4L97 – the 05.19 Trafford Park–Felixstowe, conveying a well-loaded service.

With the early morning mist clearing, No. 90044 heads south at Gordons Lodge, Ashton, on 26 August 2016, working 1M16 – the 20.44 Inverness–London Euston Caledonian sleeper service – with its mixture of Mk 2 and Mk 3 coaches.

In Freightliner early two-tone grey, still with BR arrows, No. 90145 heads south at Ashton on 26 July 2000 with 4L89 – the 03.30 Garston–Ipswich Yard service.

Sixteen years on from the previous picture, No. 90045, now in Powerhaul livery, heads 1M16 – the 20.44 Inverness–London Euston Caledonian sleeper service – through Old Lindslade on 12 August 2016.

With its climb up out of Ipswich, No. 90045 passes Belstead Bank working 4M87 – the 11.13 Felixstowe–Trafford Park service – on 28 January 2016.

Minus its bodyside Freightliner branding, No. 90046 heads north at Ashton with 4M87 – the 12.50 Ipswich Yard–Trafford Park service – on 9 August 2005.

With its consist mainly MAERSK containers, No. 90047 passes Chelmscote with 4L75 – the 09.58 Crewe Basford Hall–Felixstowe service – on 7 April 2011.

Seen in the new Freightliner Vehicle Maintenance Facility depot, on 6 October 2017, No. 90047 waits to receive attention to its wheelsets.

Heading north at Church Brampton No. 90048 passes with a short/lightly loaded 4M87 – the 11.13 Felixstowe–Trafford Park service – on 1 August 2013.

Still retaining its grey livery, No. 90048, on hire to GBRF, passes Blisworth on 24 May 2016 with 1M16 – the 20.44 Inverness–London Euston Caledonian sleeper service.

With its climb up from Northampton on 16 May 2014 a work-stained No. 90049 heads 4L97 – the 05.19 Trafford Park–Felixstowe – as it passes Courteenhall.

Powerhaul-liveried No. 90049 passes Roade, south of Northampton, with a colourful 4L41 – the 06.04 Crewe Basford Hall–Felixstowe service – on 1 July 2011.

Terminals/Yards

Freightliner uses a handful of Class 08 shunters at certain terminals such as Southampton, Trafford Park and Felixstowe, where we see No. 08531, on 26 March 2019, busy at work with the arrival of 4L89 from Coatbridge.

A busy scene at Lawley St Terminal in Birmingham on 14 May 2011 sees No. 66594 *NYK Spirit of Kyoto*, No. 66534 *OOOL Express* and No. 66533 *Hanjin Express/Senator Express* while their trains are being loaded/prepared by the terminal's new cranes, which were replaced in March 2008.

Stud Farm Quarry in Leicestershire is the setting as No. 66507 passes under the loading bunker while being loaded with track ballast, forming 6P06 to Bescot Virtual Quarry on 17 April 2003.

With Chaddesden Sidings in Derby being used as a virtual quarry for the West Coast main line upgrade, here we see No. 66603 shortly after arriving with 6P02 from Bardon Hill Quarry on 21 February 2003.

No. 66528 waits to depart Forders Sidings in Bedfordshire, on 8 April 2003, with 6C51 – the 09.38 empty bin liner to Cricklewood. Sadly, Forders closed to rail traffic in April 2005 and the working now uses the Calvert site in Buckinghamshire.

Now working for Freightliner in Poland as FLP 66011 since August 2009, No. 66584 arrives at Neasden before setting back into the Bardon Terminal with 6M17 – the 10.17 from Croft Quarry in Leicestershire on 18 July 2007.

Also working in Poland, No. 66624 is seen at the Bardon Aggregates Terminal at Thorney Mill, on 15 April 2010, while unloading 6V48 from Bardon Hill Quarry. Since this photo was taken Thorney Mill has closed and been relocated at Colnbrook.

A different view at West Thurrock Tarmac Terminal looking north with the QE2 bridge and the HS1 line. No. 66613 waits to setback out of the sidings with 6M84 – the 12.44 to Tunstead Sidings on 29 December 2016.

Tarmacs Elstow Terminal, to the south of Bedford, is the location as No. 66614 starts to unload over the BDU after arriving with 6Z37 – the 04.27 from Tunstead Sidings – on 27 April 2015.

Sadly, a day before Forders Sidings closed to refuse traffic, Freightliner's Shanks-liveried No. 66522 *East London Express* waits to depart Cricklewood Shanks Terminal with 6A64 to Forders on 7 April 2005.

With the closure of Forders Sidings in April 2005 for household waste, the North London waste was transferred to Calvert in Buckinghamshire. On 11 August 2005, No. 66622 is seen after arriving with 6M22 – the 08.21 from Cricklewood.

In late 2011 Freightliner took on the lease for ten ex-DRS Class 66s. No. 66417 was exported to Poland in February 2012 and now works for FPL in mainland Europe. Here we see the loco in Wroclaw Gadow yard, with its new identity as No. 66014, on 23 August 2014 after arriving with forty-five wagons loaded with aggregates.

No. 66553 waits to depart Croft Sidings in Leicestershire with 6M17 – the 10.17 aggregate service to Neasden, in London – on 9 March 2007.

With Freightliner having the contract to deliver the GWR Class 387s from Derby Litchurch Lane to Bletchley TMD, for mileage accumulation the company put redundant HHA coal wagons to good use as barrier vehicles for brake force. On 6 October 2017, No. 66510 waits to depart Bletchley TMD Sidings with 4K33 to Crewe Basford Hall.

Taking a break from its normal intermodal duties on 29 April 2002, No. 57010 *Freightliner Crusader* was on yard shunt duties at Crewe Basford Hall standing in replacement for the then Class 47 normally used.

Looked on by the QE2 bridge over the river Thames, No. 66605 is seen in West Thurrock Tarmac Terminal, on 16 April 2018 after arriving with 6L10 – the 21.04 loaded cement from Tunstead Sidings.

Not long after its repaint into Powerhaul colours, No. 66528 *Madge Elliot MBE (Borders Railway 2015)* is seen in Luton Crescent Road yard unloading 6C77 – the 04.11 arrival from Mountsorrel – on 19 May 2015.

A rare sight in Wolverton works on 28 March 2007 sees No. 47816 waiting to depart with Southern Railways refurbished Class 456, No. 456005, as 5Z18 to Selhurst TM&RSD.

No. 66622 is seen in the old Dagenham Down Sidings being loaded with scrap for Cardiff on 15 January 2012. With big changes and development, the site is now in the hands of Breedon cement, as seen in the next picture.

The new Breedon cement terminal at Dagenham is the setting as No. 66623, sporting its new Genesee & Wyoming colours, waits to depart with 6M84 – the 14.08 empties to Hope Earles Sidings – on 24 May 2019.

Catching the early morning sun. Crewe Basford Hall yard, on 24 July 2018, shows three different traction types used by intermodal as they all wait departures with Nos 66512, 86627 and 90049.

Acknowledgements

As I compile this book, I will be starting my eighteenth year as a driver with Freightliner Heavyhaul, after commencing at Rugby depot in 2002 and moving to Bedford depot in 2010. I have chosen a selection of pictures that cover most of Freightliner's workings today dating back to 1999. I was lucky enough to take photographs while at work, showing the company's operations, as well as early to modern day liveries on the locomotives.

I would like to thank those who have helped with information, and my fellow friend and photographer John Turner, who has assisted with filling gaps in my photograph collection. Also, thanks to the managers and work colleagues at Freightliner for their help, which is greatly appreciated.

Dave Smith
2019